Original title:
Mossy Musings

Copyright © 2025 Creative Arts Management OÜ
All rights reserved.

Author: Theodore Sinclair
ISBN HARDBACK: 978-1-80566-603-5
ISBN PAPERBACK: 978-1-80566-888-6

The Rich Palette of Nature

In a forest where colors blend,
The trees gossip, the leaves pretend.
Squirrels wear hats, they dance with flair,
Even the flowers seem to share a dare.

A rabbit's got style, with shoes so bright,
He hops past the birch in a zig-zag flight.
The sun, a painter, splashes with glee,
Nature's a circus — oh, come join me!

Hidden Lives in the Dew

Along the grass, the dew drops gleam,
Tiny worlds waking, a daylight dream.
A spider whispers, "Just don't look down!"
While ants parade, wearing tiny crowns.

A ladybug mumbles, "Why wear the red?"
When plaid would suit her little head.
Beneath the leaves, the secrets brew,
Oh, the mischief that hides in the dew!

Nature's Textured Soliloquy

The bark of the tree tells age-old tales,
Of critters that scamper and gusty gales.
A worm in a turtleneck struts with pride,
While a snail in loafers takes it slow, with stride.

Moss on the stones whispers, "Take a rest,"
While the rocks grumble, "Hey, we're the best!"
Textures alive in this leafy comical play,
Nature's own laughter brightens the day.

Color of Stillness

In shades of green, the quiet sits,
With dandelions planning clever skits.
A frog in tuxedo takes center stage,
"Who knew I'd be a nature sage?"

Butterflies giggle, swap tales of flight,
While owls roll their eyes, "What a sight!"
Stillness surrounds, but oh what a noise,
In nature's palette, we find our joys!

In Shadows of Growth

In shady glens where grasses tease,
The mushrooms dance upon the breeze.
A squirrel slips, then gives a shout,
"Why wear a cape if I can't sprout!"

The trees conspire with whispered glee,
As snails race past a sleeping bee.
"You think you're fast?" the grass blades croak,
But speed's no match for a snail's joke!

Beneath the oaks, a troop of bugs,
Engage in fights with little shrugs.
"Your smell's too sweet, it's making me sneeze!"
And then they all just laugh with ease.

Nature's antics in vibrant hues,
Where laughter sprouts like morning dews.
In shadows deep, life finds a way,
To sparkle in its funny play.

Soft Padding of Nature

The ferns wear hats the sun forgot,
While raindrops fall like tiny dots.
A raccoon scampers, loses its grip,
And lands with a plop, oh what a trip!

The squirrels, they giggle as they spy,
A sloth, who thinks it's passing by.
"Step up your game, you sleepy dude!"
Then, back to munching on their food.

A puddle gleams like a disco ball,
Reflecting crunches from the waterfall.
The frogs dive in with leaps and bounds,
Creating ripples; oh, what sounds!

With every step, the earth lets out,
A squishy laugh, a joyful shout.
In soft padding, nature's wit,
Is found in every little bit.

A Symphony of Spheres

Tiny acorns roll with flair,
While whirligigs twirl through the air.
A raccoon's party, yes, it's grand,
With nuts and seeds all by demand!

The butterflies take to the skies,
Doing pirouettes, oh how they rise!
A beetle conducts from the branch,
Shouting, "Join in! Come take a chance!"

The wind plays strings of softest breath,
While all around, there's life, not death.
Rainbows giggle, the clouds all sway,
In this orchestra where critters play.

With every note, the trees applaud,
As laughter echoes through the broad.
A symphony beneath the green,
Nature's concert, sweet and keen.

Dwelling in Dampness

In the dampness, a worm sings low,
To raindrops tapping on the meadow.
"I'm wriggling here, what's your excuse?"
A frog responds, "To find my muse!"

The mushrooms sport their squishy hats,
While beetles brag about their spats.
"You think you're tough on soggy ground?"
"I'm hard as nails!" the toad bellowed sound.

Puddles reflect the sky's sly wink,
Bubbles burst as frogs stop to think.
A snail slides past, oh what a show!
"I'll get there first, just watch me go!"

Dampness dances and weaves with cheer,
Creating joy for all who peer.
Nature's antics, never bland,
In this wet world, life strikes a band.

Cradle of the Understory

In the shade where critters play,
Fungi dance and giggle all day.
A squirrel jokes with a singing tree,
While wise old owls just sip their tea.

Lichens whisper secrets on bark,
A beetle sports a glowing spark.
They host a party, wild and free,
With mushrooms twirling joyfully!

Illuminated by Dappled Light

In sunlight's patches, shadows tease,
A rabbit mocks a buzzing bee.
"Catch me if you can!" it boasts with glee,
While hoppy friends roll back in trees.

Frogs critique the wobbly worms,
"Your dance needs style," the pond bug squirms.
The sunbeams giggle, join the fun,
As insects serenade everyone!

Contemplation on a Log

A turtle sits, his thoughts in flight,
"Why rush?" he muses, "I'm just alright."
His friends all mock, say, "Get a move!"
Yet he just chuckles, finds his groove.

The raccoon jokes, "What's life's big deal?
Is it meals or naps that make us real?"
As critters ponder, time ticks slow,
Silly debates in nature's show!

Ruminations by a Stream

The water flows with giggles and glee,
A fish whispers, "Hey, look at me!"
With splashes loud and bubbles bright,
They splash each other in sheer delight.

A frog croaks loud, "This game's the best!"
While snails take bets on who'll outrest.
Rippling laughter fills the air,
As nature's children banter and care!

Contemplative Greenery

In the shade where ferns do sway,
I ponder life in a leafy way.
A snail takes its leisurely glide,
While ants have their plans to confide.

A dandelion wishes to fly,
But sticks to the ground—oh my, oh my!
Its dreams get tangled in knotted weeds,
Yet still it grows with tiny seeds.

The Hushed Voice of Nature

The trees whisper secrets untold,
In their trunks, wisdom grows old.
A squirrel with nutty designs,
Coaxes the sun to peek through pines.

The breeze giggles, tickles the brook,
While bugs draw maps in the open nook.
If only rabbits could read their plans,
They'd win the race from bankers' hands!

Treading on Soft Surfaces

Each step sinks into emerald dreams,
Where shaded paths aren't what they seem.
The Earth beneath feels slightly spongy,
As if it teases, 'Come on, befunny.'

A frog croaks humor from the dew,
With a punchline that hops right at you.
His jokes might not make sense today,
But in the woods, who cares, I say!

Breath of the Earth

The ground inhales in solemn glee,
With wiggly worms enjoying the spree.
Each blade of grass grins wide and bright,
As sunlight dances, a pure delight.

The daisies chuckle, 'We're pretty profound,'
While dandelions scatter all around.
Just stop and laugh with the soil's embrace,
For life is a joke in this cozy space.

A Dance of Shadows and Dreams

In a glen where shadows play,
The water sprite tripped on the clay.
With every step, she squeaked with glee,
Her friends just laughed, 'Oh, look at she!'

The trees all whispered, secrets bright,
As fireflies twinkled, lighting the night.
A squirrel spun tales of acorn gold,
While a sleepy owl hooted, rather bold.

Dance on, dear shadows, don't be shy,
With twirling leaves and a wink to the sky.
A rabbit, too, joined the frolicking fray,
Joking about the berries on display.

In this silly waltz under the moon,
Even crickets joined in with a tune.
As giggles echoed through the dark,
The night held laughter, light as a lark.

Secrets of the Sublime

In the garden where gossip grows,
The flowers gossip, who knows?
'Did you see that butterfly flop?'
As they elbowed, their petals would pop.

A snail slipped by, thinking profound,
'Do I look slow, or am I just round?'
The daisies chuckled, 'You're quite the catch,'
He smiled and replied, 'Yeah, I know, I'm a sketch!'

With ladybugs chatting about their spots,
The ants lined up for their funny plots.
They whispered why mushrooms always dance,
It seems they had too much luck in romance!

In this sublime space of giggles and cheer,
Nature's odd secrets are tucked, oh so near.
So join in the laughter, don't be demure,
In the silly kingdom, happiness is pure!

Emerald Whisperings

In vivid greens, a frog takes a leap,
'Watch my jumps!' he croaks, 'Not one that's cheap!'
The leaves chuckle, swaying with style,
'You call that a hop? Wait, see my guile!'

A wiggly worm joins the croaking laugh,
'When I dance, folks scream and chaff!'
The daisies wink, 'Well, that's quite bold,
But let's be honest, you look rather cold!'

The moss collected tales from the dew,
'We've seen some jumps, but none like you!'
Giggling softly, it shared with the sun,
'Each slip and slide just adds to the fun.'

So the emerald friends twirled beneath the skies,
In a green-tinted laughter, the earth's happy cries.
Together they sang, nature's sweet choir,
In the vibrant realm of mirth and mirth-fire.

Beneath the Canopy

Under the trees where giggles reside,
A hedgehog rolled by, filled with pride.
'I'm the fastest creature on this block,'
The squirrels just snickered, 'You're more like a rock!'

A chatter of birds had a counting game,
'How many worms fit in a frame?'
The worms, all snug, slowly just sighed,
'Counting is tough when so well-tied.'

In this refuge of whimsy and cheer,
The canopy giggled, oh so dear.
Shadows played tricks, all teasingly bright,
As nature spun stories with pure delight.

So gather around, in this jolly retreat,
Where animals dance and all tales are sweet.
In the rustling leaves, find joy that won't quit,
Beneath the canopy, laughter's a hit!

Secrets of the Forest Floor

Beneath the trees, they laugh and play,
Tiny critters in a leafy ballet.
Squirrels gossip in acorn hats,
While mushrooms dance with the chattiest rats.

A snail confesses to a wise old tree,
"Why did I race? It's clear to see,
Slow and steady wins the day,
But I'm just sliming the fun away!"

A spider spins tales of past mishaps,
Of caught-up flies and sticky traps.
The ants march on, a brigade of cheer,
"We'll take the crumbs; don't shed a tear!"

Under a log, all secrets blend,
Each shadow whispers, and laughter won't end.
So come take a peek and join the spree,
In the cheerful hush of the forest's decree.

Verdant Reveries

In the glade where clovers cluster tight,
A frog hits a note that feels just right.
With every ribbit, the bugs join in,
A chorus of nature, let the giggles begin.

The woodpecker drums with a rhythmic flair,
"Knock, knock! Who's there?" rings in the air.
Each tree holds tales of whimsical times,
Where vines play hopscotch, and mossy sings chimes.

A hedgehog rolls, what a tangled mess,
"Can someone help me? I wish to impress!"
Beneath the ferns, secrets take flight,
As laughter escapes into the warming light.

The forest joins in a merry charade,
Where the sun's both a wink and a parade.
Lose yourself in this jolly retreat,
Where every step feels like a dance to your beat.

Lush Memories of Green

Under the leaves, stories sprout,
With laughter that trickles without a doubt.
The beetles boast of their shiny shields,
As rabbits play poker on dandelion fields.

A wise old owl with glasses perched low,
Cautions against gossip, or so he will crow.
"Judge not the toad for his bumpy skin,
He's really quite charming, let the fun begin!"

The daisies giggle, their heads held high,
At the poor worm who dreams of the sky.
"You're grounded now, but space is vast,
One day you'll soar, just give it a cast!"

And the breeze carries whispers, wild and free,
The forest is full of hilarity.
So join the dance where dreams intertwine,
In tales of wonder, and laughter divine.

The Tapestry of Tranquility

Amidst the roots, a party awaits,
With mushrooms as chairs and frogs as mates.
A raccoon dines on imaginary pie,
Shouting, "Bring cake! We're soaring high!"

The sunbeams peek through the swaying leaves,
While peacocks strut in their finest weaves.
Old bushes chuckle at the silly sights,
As bumblebees buzz about plump delights.

A fox in a hat tells riddles galore,
"Why cross the road? There's fun to explore!"
Swaying in rhythm, each animal sings,
In a vibrant tapestry of joyful things.

So linger and laugh in this jovial nook,
Where silence can giggle, and stillness can cook.
Within this forest, the charm is so bright,
That even the stars giggle with delight.

The Lullaby of Lichen

In a world where whispers grow,
Lichens sing with gentle flow.
They sway on stones, a cozy sight,
In their green world, all feels right.

Beneath the trees, they hold a dance,
Tickling fancy with each glance.
They giggle soft as breezes tease,
A playful bunch, at heart, they please.

With colors bright, they paint the path,
Unruly sprouts with joyous math.
Their laughter echoes, sweet and clear,
Inviting all to come and cheer.

In cozy corners where they thrive,
A secret joke that keeps them alive.
The lichen laugh, oh what a thrill,
A turf of glee on every hill.

Forgotten Ferns' Haiku

Forgotten in the shade,
Whispered tales of ferns parade,
Dancing leaves in jokes made.

In the shadow's gentle clasp,
Nature's giggles softly grasp,
Even ferns know how to rasp.

They tickle toes, the garden seat,
With wise cracks that can't be beat,
A green carpet beneath your feet.

Nature's Plush Embrace

Nature's blanket, soft and wide,
With leafy laughter, dreams abide.
A plush embrace, so sly, so bright,
Where each moment feels just right.

Critters bound with squeaky zest,
Soft paths that lead to playful rest.
With every leaf a little grin,
The forest's humor draws you in.

Twisting roots in silly shapes,
They hold secrets, make escapes.
In soft cocoon where joy delights,
Nature giggles through the nights.

The Silent Softness

In stillness, humor softly creeps,
Whispering tales that nature keeps.
The quiet giggles of the trees,
Chuckle gently in the breeze.

Each mossy stone, a silent muse,
Winks at you with earthy views.
A cuddly world, plush and serene,
With jesters dressed in leafy green.

In nooks where shadows dance and play,
The subtle jokes take flight each day.
Softness hiding sneaky glee,
The earth's delight, just wait and see.

Gentle Green Reveries

In the forest, where green dreams play,
Tiny creatures laugh and sway.
A snail slips by with style so grand,
Wearing the tiniest hat on hand.

The mushrooms giggle in the light,
Winking with glee, what a sight!
A frog croaks jokes, crackling clear,
While ants march on, with no fear.

The breeze carries whispers of cheer,
As squirrels cause chaos, oh dear!
Nature's comedy unfolds with grace,
In the green and vibrant space.

So, take a moment, breathe it in,
Join the laughter, let joy begin.
For in this realm of leafy delight,
Every day brings a new highlight.

Dreaming of Earth's Embrace

In a meadow where daisies twirl,
A sleepy worm gives its best whirl.
Dancing slowly, lost in a trance,
While ants break into a funny dance.

The sun peeks in with a bright hello,
Tickling the leaves to make them glow.
A squirrel trips, making quite the sound,
As acorns tumble to the ground.

Grasshoppers join in as a band,
With crickets clapping, oh so grand!
Each hop and chirp in perfect time,
Nature's humor, so sublime.

Dreaming away under skies so blue,
With starlit stories, fresh and new.
Hold tight to this strange, funny space,
Where laughter sprinkles the entire place.

Chronicles of the Forest Floor

Upon the forest floor, stories unfold,
Of creatures mischievous and bold.
A raccoon wears a mask so sly,
While beetles march, oh my, oh my!

Fungi giggle, spreading their cheer,
As moss-covered rocks lend an ear.
The leaves rustle secrets so grand,
Whispering tales of the forest band.

A hedgehog prances, spiky and proud,
Turning heads in the gossiping crowd.
With tiny shoes and a jolly air,
He rolls about without a care.

Each step a poem, each turn a riddle,
Life in the woods strums a quirky fiddle.
So listen closely, pick up the lore,
For life on the ground is hard to ignore.

Nature's Quiet Commentary

In the shade of trees, wisdom flows,
As squirrels observe people in prose.
A turtle, slow, takes its sweet time,
As a bluebird sings in perfect rhyme.

The air is thick with stories untold,
As nature chuckles, brave and bold.
A ladybug twirls on a leaf so green,
Noticing life in every scene.

A bear looks on, munching some berries,
Imagining humans with their worries.
With a scratch of fur, it lets out a yawn,
Wondering why they rush at dawn.

Nature's quiet, yet speaks so loud,
In giggles and nudges from each shroud.
So pause for a moment, look around,
And delight in the joy that can be found.

Gossamer Thoughts on Green

In the garden, thoughts do dance,
A ladybug leads with a prance.
Worms in bow ties spin and twirl,
While flower petals take a whirl.

Butterflies gossip, sipping nectar,
Saying, 'Who's the real collector?'
Grass blades giggle, tickling feet,
As squirrels debate which nut's a treat.

Frogs croak rhymes in their croaky tune,
While ants march by, in a funny platoon.
The daisies nod in joyful cheer,
Nature's stage is quite sincere.

And as the sun begins to set,
I find myself quite lost in wit.
The world is funny, there's no doubt,
In this green realm where joy stands out.

Seeking Serenity in Shade

Beneath a tree, I sit and plot,
Dreaming of snacks I have forgot.
The breeze tells tales of things unseen,
While squirrels act like royalty, keen.

A wooden bench groans with my weight,
Saying, 'Hurry up, don't tempt fate!'
And while the sun beats down with might,
I giggle at ants in their small fight.

Birds serenade with songs so bright,
While grasshoppers leap—oh, what a sight!
Each shade of green whispers a tale,
Of laughter woven within the veil.

Yet, all I want is ice cream near,
A thought that brings me such good cheer.
I watch the world from this sweet glade,
Where every chuckle simply won't fade!

Life Close to the Ground

Creeping low, where treasures hide,
Ants hold conferences, dignified.
In this patch of grass, what spies I see,
A beetle in sneakers, bold as can be.

Caterpillars munch their leafy feast,
Proclaiming themselves the 'Leafy Beast.'
While flocks of bugs share their latest craze,
Fashion tips in the sunlight rays.

I spy a snail, slow and serene,
Sporting a shell, oh so keen!
He says, 'Life isn't just a pace,
It's more about style, and less about race.'

Underfoot, the world's a stage,
Where tiny critters pen each page.
With every giggle, I do vow,
To get down low, and join them now!

Whispers of Ancient Growth

In the woods, secrets emerge,
From tree trunks, stories converge.
Fungus boasts of its fine cuisine,
While shadows giggle, vibrant and green.

Old roots stretch out, grasping the ground,
Moss-covered tales where laughter's found.
A raccoon in glasses reads with glee,
The latest news from the old oak tree.

Twists and knots in branches that sway,
Holding parlor games in their own way.
Each rustle brings a chuckle or two,
In the wisdom of nature, bold and true.

And here I sit, a curious friend,
Embracing whimsy that knows no end.
With every whisper, humor grows,
In nature's heart, where laughter flows.

Whispers of the Forest Floor

Beneath the trees, the secrets creep,
A choir of leaves, they never sleep.
Squirrels gossip, nuts in hand,
While shadows dance in their own band.

Fungi chuckle, their caps are bright,
While bunny rabbits leap in flight.
The ladybugs have quite the show,
In tiny tuxedos, they steal the glow.

When sunlight tickles the ground so sweet,
The ants march by on tiny feet.
Frogs croak jokes, they're quite the jest,
In nature's comedy, they are blessed.

Lichen's Lullaby

On rocks where soft green blankets stay,
Lichens whisper and softly play.
They tell of times, both old and grand,
Of stories spun and time unplanned.

In patches bright, they jest and tease,
While moss looks on, intent to freeze.
A snail slips by, a slow ballet,
Waving to friends at the end of the day.

With every raindrop, laughter swells,
As slugs revel in their slimy spells.
A dance of life beneath the gloom,
In this green theater, all find room.

Beneath the Velvet Canopy

The trees wear coats of emerald hue,
Where critters frolic and sit askew.
With every gust, the branches sway,
Nature's riddle brightens the day.

A chipmunk cracks a nut with flair,
While fireflies twinkle like they just don't care.
With acorn hats upon their heads,
They throw a party, no dull treads!

A wise old owl in the crook of a bough,
Eavesdrops on tales, "Oh, tell me how!"
The laughter echoes, faint but clear,
In this forest, everyone's dear.

Secrets of the Soft Earth

In the loamy depths where secrets lie,
Worms spin tales and snails reply.
Grubs giggle with dirt on their face,
As roots entangle in the soft embrace.

A tiny mole, with dreams so grand,
Decides to build his kingdom of sand.
While beetles march, a parade absurd,
Each one a knight, with armor stirred.

The ground squirrels gossip, round and round,
In their underground, there's joy abound.
With every burrow, a story's told,
In the soft earth's heart, adventures unfold.

The Green Veil of Inspiration

Underneath the leafy dome,
Thoughts wander like a gnome.
Inspiration hides so sly,
Waiting for the curious eye.

Shadows play their little tricks,
Pretending life's a bag of bricks.
With a giggle, I agree,
To join the fun with glee.

The sunlight tickles every hue,
Whispers secrets, old yet new.
I dance with ferns, a merry spree,
A verdant world just laughs with me.

In every nook a joke resides,
Where laughter and the green abide.
So here beneath this nature's veil,
Let's share a laugh and tell a tale.

Recollections in Shade

In the shade where memories lie,
I spot a squirrel dash on by.
Was that a friend or just a tease?
I laugh at branches bending breeze.

Old stories cling to bumpy bark,
Whisper nonsense, make a mark.
The more I ponder, the more it seems,
That laughter booms in leafy dreams.

Who planted those shoes in a crook?
They're handy if you like to cook!
Perhaps they danced, or ran away,
I'll join the fun, come what may.

Here's to all the tales unsung,
Where every whisper leaves us young.
So, raise a glass to shade so sweet,
With funny thoughts and leafy feet.

Threads of Verdancy

In a world of threads so green,
I find the silliest unseen.
A vine creeps up to tie my shoe,
Saying, "Wouldn't you like to woo?"

With every twist, a giggle grows,
A tapestry of nature's prose.
I weave my thoughts in sunny spins,
While tangled roots just start to grin.

The petals wink, the bugle plays,
I hear their laughter in the rays.
"Hurry up!", the daisies cheer,
Join us now, the fun is here!

So here's a toast to verdant laughs,
To playful roots and leafy halves.
I'll prance around till daylight's end,
In nature's threads, my jolly friend.

A Tranquil Abode Amongst Leaves

In a cozy nook where laughter blooms,
I found a haven in leafy rooms.
The whispers of the trees are loud,
As if they're speaking to the crowd.

With every rustle, giggles align,
A comfy chair in the sunshine.
"Stay awhile, don't rush," they plead,
As I settle down for some green tea creed.

In this abode of cuddly sights,
Jokes flutter by like crazy kites.
"Did you see that worm's cute little wig?"
A tiny dance makes laughter big.

So here amidst the trunks and leaves,
I craft a tale that never leaves.
Where tranquility meets giddy fun,
In nature's arms, we laugh, we run.

Beneath the Canopy of Contemplation

A squirrel in a bowler hat,
Debates with a wise old cat.
"Why climb so high?" the feline purrs,
"When down here, life's just full of whirs!"

A raccoon with spectacles on,
Reads tales beneath the fading dawn.
He chuckles softly, "What a plot!"
As acorns dance—oh, what a lot!

The shadows shuffle, play their games,
As chipmunks join in with funny names.
"Let's have a giggle, let's make a scene,
Your nutty dreams shall be our queen!"

So laughter echoes, rich and bold,
Through leafy laughs both new and old.
When pondering life, it's clear to see,
The forest jesters are wild and free!

Whispered Wishes in the Understory

In a thicket, a rumor spreads,
"Are the mushrooms talking in their beds?"
Little critters gather near,
For tales spun softly, full of cheer.

Beneath the ferns, a hedgehog sighs,
"Do whispers count as goodbyes?"
A passing turtle calls back, "No way!
We'll chirp our secrets every day!"

The beetles boast of their grand flights,
While fireflies twinkle, sparking lights.
"Come take a ride!" the ladybug grins,
"As we search for treasure beneath our skins!"

Oh, laughter dances in the gloam,
As mushrooms weave their tales at home.
In shadows, wishes take their chance,
For life, it seems, is one big dance!

The Forgotten Fables of the Forest

Once, in the woods, a fox wore shoes,
He waltzed and pranced, shared clever views.
"Chasing tails is a silly affair,
So let's discuss who wears what hair!"

A wise old owl shook his head,
"Forget your shoes, just use your tread!
Life's not measured in peppy strides,
But in the laughter that abides!"

The turtles told a tale or two,
Of races won by the smallest crew.
"Slow and steady wins the race!"
And laughter echoed, filling space.

So gather round and share a jest,
In nature's arms, we're surely blessed.
These fables weave through every glade,
In whispers shared, the joy won't fade!

The Hidden Life of Leafy Layers

Beneath the leaves, a party brews,
As ants debate the biggest shoes.
"Size does matter!" one ant shouts,
While others laugh and dance about.

A beetle dressed in flashy threads,
Spins tales of glory, wide-spread.
"Who knew my shell could shine so bright,
In the glow of this leafy night?"

Grasshoppers hop with funny zest,
"Come join our band, it's simply the best!
We'll serenade the passing breeze,
As fireflies flicker with giggles and wheeze!"

So, under layers, laughter unfurls,
In this hidden life where joy swirls.
Through whimsical rhymes and playful sights,
Nature's comedy takes its flights!

Where Green Dreams Dwell

In a patch of green where snails are slow,
The gnomes have a party, and the mushrooms glow.
They dance in the shade, sipping dew from a cup,
And the fireflies giggle as they light up the sup.

The rabbits wear hats, quite stylish and neat,
While hedgehogs waltz with a whimsical beat.
A squirrel juggles acorns, it's quite a sight!
In this leafy kingdom, all's merry and bright.

The grasshoppers sing with voices so grand,
Conducted by crickets, a lyrical band.
While owls in bow ties look down with a grin,
In this place of delight, let the fun begin!

Dreams linger here where the wild things play,
Where laughter is found in the softest of hay.
So join in the frolic, don't just stand still,
In a world full of whimsy, let's never lose thrill!

A Quiet Green Sanctuary

In the heart of the woods, where the ferns like to twirl,
A tortoise named Timmy has dreams to unfurl.
He's planning a party with snacks made of leaves,
While the raccoons giggle and plot in the eaves.

A ladybug sings to a worm with a fedora,
As beetles parade in a glittering aura.
The invitations flutter, just look at them glide,
As the earthworms wiggle, they take it in stride.

A gathering festive, with laughter and cheer,
Where the daisies gossip, all ears to the sphere.
Each critter has stories and jokes that they tell,
It's a sanctuary bright, where all creatures dwell.

So come join the fun in this green forest nook,
With surprises quite vivid, just take a good look.
In the quiet of nature, absurdity blooms,
As the creatures make magic, and joy consumes!

Whispers of the Woodland

In whispers of leaves, the squirrels conspire,
To keep all the secrets, their mischievous fire.
With a nutty delight, they play hide and seek,
While the owls keep watch with a wise, softened peek.

The ferns wave hello to the passing sunray,
As the toads have a karaoke night, come what may.
Croaking out tunes with a froggy flair,
In the laughter of frogs, no worries to bear.

The fox in his scarf tells tall tales of spots,
While the chipmunks giggle, tying shoelace knots.
A game of leapfrog, oh what a delight,
In the whispers of woodland, the world feels just right.

So gather your friends, bring a snack or two,
In this bustling, bright haven, the whole forest crew.
With each fluttering leaf, the laughter will swell,
In the whimsical air where the woodland does dwell!

Embrace of the Earth

On the rich, earthy floor where the mushrooms grow,
A parade of odd critters is putting on a show.
The bugs wear their costumes, all funny and bright,
While the grass tickles toes, it's a jubilant sight.

With a laugh and a leap, the frogs do their best,
To perfect their ballet, a wobbly fest.
The hedgehogs cheer loudly with pom-poms made of moss,
In this strange little world, do we win or just toss?

The fox with a wink hosts a riddle so sly,
While the bees buzz along, creating the hype.
A turtle breaks barriers, moves faster than light,
It's a hub of pure joy, everything feels right.

So dance with the pebbles, and sing with the trees,
Join the embrace of the earth, if you please.
In this realm of enchantment, the fun never ends,
Where laughter floats freely, and nature transcends!

Emerald Dreams in Dappled Light

In a forest so lush, where the shadows play,
Squirrels debate on who will save the day.
A snail took a ride on a leaf that was wide,
And claimed he was swift - now that's quite a stride!

Beneath the tall ferns, a rabbit does sing,
Hoping one day, he'll be crowned forest king.
He dreams of a throne made of clover and grass,
But his royal decree is just more carrots to amass!

A wise old owl, perched high in the spruce,
Tells tales of the days when the trees had a truce.
He chuckles aloud as the pinecones all fall,
"We pines were once kings until acorns had a ball!"

And so in this glade, where giggles abound,
Nature spins tales that are joyful, unbound.
With critters so silly, under sun and shade,
Emerald dreams dance in the laughter they made.

Verdant Reflections

Green leaves gossip under the bright, sunny ray,
While ants in a line are dramatically gay.
They march in a fashion most grand and absurd,
With all of their chatter, one thinks they're a herd!

A frog in the pond tries to float on a log,
He slips and he slides, what a sight for a frog!
He croaks out a joke to the fish swimming by,
"Why fit in water when a splash is more sly?"

In tufts of soft grass, a ladybug jokes,
As she sips on nectar, surrounded by blokes.
"My spots are my fashion, so never you fret,
In the world of style, I'm the best in the set!"

With the chuckles of flowers and whispers of trees,
Nature's a comedy, bringing us ease.
In verdant reflections, hum with glee,
And let the wild laughter flow free as the breeze.

The Silent Green Beneath

Beneath the tall oaks, where the shadows grow,
A critter convenes with his friends down below.
They giggle and chat about seeds and the rain,
While plotting a dance that will drive humans insane!

A caterpillar claims he'll soon learn to fly,
His pals roll their eyes and chuckle nearby.
"You've got to cocoon, before soaring above,
And maybe then, Benny, you'll find you have love!"

A mole with a motto, "It's dark but it's grand,"
Hums tunes for the critters who tap in the sand.
He swears living low is the greatest delight,
While the rabbit above just hops out of sight!

And so in the depths, where it's silent and true,
Life's odd little jesters dream under the dew.
With quirks and a wink, they share laughter and mirth,
In the silent green below, oh what a place of worth!

Nature's Cushion

With petals of velvet and grass soft as pie,
The critters set up for a grand picnic, oh my!
They nibble on acorns while gossiping loud,
As sunbeams dance down on this merry little crowd.

A hedgehog in shades sips his tea with delight,
He dives for a crumb that just danced out of sight.
"If I'm in a jam, I can roll with the best!"
He chuckles so bright, feeling truly blessed.

A worm brings a joke that gets some giggles and snorts,
"I'm great at digressing, even in short reports!"
And everyone's laughing, as shadows stretch wide,
While ants serve the snacks with such joyful pride.

Nature's cushion is vibrant, a quilt born of fun,
Where every small creature can bask in the sun.
With laughter as charm and delights all around,
This whimsical world is where joy can be found.

The Poetry of Patina

In corners where dust bunnies dance,
Old memories sit, but don't take a chance.
With spoons gone rogue and forks in the trees,
Patina whispers, 'Oh, please just sneeze!'

A teapot chuckles, green tea gone cold,
It tells tales of kittens that never grow old.
Each drip at the spout sings a raucous tune,
While dust settles softly like whispers of June.

Old shoes on the shelf seek a night on the town,
With laces untied as they tumble down.
They giggle through echoes of laughter and glee,
And waltz like the stars in the grand old marquee.

In layers so thick, history sways,
With each bump and wrinkle, it merrily plays.
So raise up your green goblet, toast to the grime,
For the poetry's rich, and it's all out of time.

Life Threaded Through Time

A thread of green runs through my day,
Guiding my footsteps in a whimsical play.
It wiggles and wobbles like a playful old cat,
Dancing with joy in a vintage top hat.

Buttons from jackets tell stories of yore,
A garden of laughter under the floor.
Whispers of daisies, as bees start to hum,
They giggle about the drumming of the thumb.

Every old trinket, a tale to unfold,
With laughs echoing softly, never too bold.
Life stitches the past with a needle of fun,
While time ticks along, never on the run.

In the tapestry woven with moments so bright,
The laughter of ages bids us goodnight.
So let's raise a mug, let our spirits align,
For life's a grand quilt, and we're all intertwined.

Green Enchantment's Embrace

A fern in the corner, a comedian grand,
Whispers to daisies, lends them a hand.
With laughter like bubbles, they dance in the breeze,
While old garden gnomes exchange silly decrees.

Toadstools wear hats that are floppy and large,
Sunning themselves, they're in charge of the charge.
With giggles and wiggles, they spread their delight,
Inviting the insects to join in the night.

Oh, the chuckles of crickets, how merry they sing,
Underneath roses with new copper rings.
A patch of green dreams where the sun likes to play,
Wrapping up secrets in fantastic display.

So let's raise a toast to the whims of the leaves,
For nature's musicians, in laughter, believe.
In this enchanted embrace, oh so spry,
We'll dance with the shadows that frolic nearby.

The Gentle Touch of Time

Oh, the tickle of time, like a feather's soft sigh,
A toast with the teacups held under the sky.
With wrinkles that giggle and swirls that amaze,
Time takes us dancing in comical ways.

The clocks like to chuckle as they tick-tock along,
Rewinding old stories, a whimsical song.
With memories bouncing like frogs on the line,
Every leap full of laughter, oh what a design!

Old wooden chairs creak as if telling a jest,
While wise squirrels chatter, just doing their best.
For every sweet moment that's gentle and bright,
Time sketches its laughter in the glow of night.

So let's laugh with the shadows, and dance in the gleam,
For life's just a whirlwind, a twirl in a dream.
In the gentle embrace where all laughter chimes,
We find our sweet rhythm, our dance with the climes.

Spirals in the Sunlight

Sunshine twirls with a cheeky grin,
Grass hitches a ride, let the fun begin.
Bugs wear shades, strut like stars,
Dance on petals, all day they spar.

Dandelions giggle, they puff and drift,
Wind joins the party, gives nature a lift.
Clouds play hide and seek with the rays,
Frogs croak jokes in their own silly ways.

Squirrels trade acorns for laughter and cheer,
Secrets exchanged between critters so near.
Nature's a riot, with quirks on display,
In spirals of sunlight, they frolic and play.

Every wild whisper invites us to smile,
Join in the fun, stay a while!
With spirals and giggles, life's a delight,
Under the sun, everything feels right.

The Quiet Pulse of the Woods

In the woods, where the trees wear capes,
Silent giggles escape little shapes.
Leaves rustle softly, what do they say?
Probably plotting a game of charades!

A squirrel in glasses reads a tall tale,
Bears do their yoga, they won't fail.
Mice play chess with a crumb for a pawn,
While owls pretend to be serious at dawn.

Mushrooms hold parties and mushrooms look great,
Dance to the rhythm that nature creates.
Chipmunks in capes swing from the vines,
Cheering for laughter, the woods intertwines.

The pulse of the woods, a giggy surprise,
Frog choirs perform under twilight skies.
In the quiet, there's humor, it's found,
Where the pulse of the woods is joyfully bound.

Echoes of Earth's Embrace

Crickets compose a symphony at night,
As fireflies twinkle, a whimsical sight.
Roots tell stories in whispers so bold,
While stones sit back, sharing secrets of old.

The hills chuckle under a sky so blue,
As shadows stretch out, they play peek-a-boo.
Worms wiggle about, getting all the laughs,
While daisies gossip in floral class.

Echoes of laughter bounce off the trees,
While ants wear tiny hats and tease.
Leaves drop low, trying to join the fun,
In Earth's warm embrace, where joy has begun.

Every step in this place is pure bliss,
With giggles and whispers, you can't miss.
Nature's a playground, full of surprise,
Echoes of Earth fill the brightening skies.

Enchanted by Green Shadows

Under the ferns where the giggles collide,
Lizards hold court, their tails open wide.
Wiggly worms tell bad jokes on a rock,
While turtles play poker around the clock.

In shadows of green, a party's afoot,
Mice wear bowties, and rabbits all hoot.
Behind leafy curtains, a chorus comes in,
With petals as shakers, they spin and grin.

The breeze plays the harp, a soft little tune,
As mushrooms moonwalk beneath the bright moon.
A hedgehog recites poetry, wild and profound,
In enchanted green shadows, laughter resounds.

Time pauses a moment, all worries take flight,
With cheeky critters making everything bright.
In nature's own theater, join in the show,
With enchanted shadows, let good humor flow.

The Essence of Earthly Grace

In the forest, voices whisper,
Trees giggle, leaves abluster.
Critters prance with socks askew,
Nature's dance, quite askew.

The earth drinks tea with honeyed glee,
While squirrels plot a grand marquee.
They argue over acorn hats,
As bees join in to chat with bats.

Laughter bubbles in the brook,
Where frogs read Shakespeare from a nook.
The air is filled with joyous sight,
In this wonderland, day to night.

With flowers singing in a band,
The flora knows, it's ever planned.
A dance of roots, they twirl around,
In this mirthful underground.

Dappled Dreams

In the glade, shadows do sway,
Mice wear tutus, hippos play.
Sunlight giggles through the leaves,
Tickling all with joyful thieves.

Dandelions hold a fair,
Where rabbits sport their fluffy hair.
Bunnies leap in capers bold,
Trading tales of carrots told.

Clouds float by, some sly, some shy,
Winking down, oh my, oh my!
They jest with bees, share secret jest,
Nature's humor, simply the best!

The wind whispers, "Come have fun!"
As ladybugs in races run.
Each blade of grass a support crew,
Cheering on the frolic too.

Carpeting the Forgotten

Underfoot, a plush surprise,
Where forgotten worries lie.
Leaves chuckle quiet little tales,
Of mossy joys beneath the gales.

In shady corners, echoes blend,
Toadstools laugh, and fairies send.
They spin about with giddy zest,
While old logs host the lively fest.

Crickets croon, "What's this? A dance?"
As fireflies flaunt their furtive prance.
Caught in whispers, secrets flit,
The forest floor, a quiet hit.

With every footstep, tales arise,
In nature's covert, boundless skies.
Where laughter reigns, and joy won't flee,
The world's carpet, wild and free.

Nature's Subtle Mentality

In the heart of the tangled wood,
Ideas sprout like they should.
Cacti wear spectacles, quite spry,
While owls make puns as they fly.

Trees hold council, their creaky chairs,
Discussing woes and woodland cares.
With barky jokes 'bout the weather,
They laugh together, light as a feather.

In denser thicket, moles conspire,
To topple pebbles, thrill, and retire.
Each ripple of laughter, a seed of glee,
Sprouting budding joy just like a spree.

Even the rocks can crack a grin,
Watching the dandelions spin.
For nature's quirks are great and vast,
In this delightful, charming cast.

The Alchemy of Moss

In the garden, where green things creep,
The chemistry of life takes a leap.
A wizard's hat made of fuzzy green,
Crafting magic where it's often unseen.

Toads in top hats, snails in a race,
Dancing around with such elegant grace.
While mushrooms giggle, a gnome takes a bow,
'Who knew this spot would be such a wow?'

Every pebble's a treasure, every leaf's a giggle,
While the squirrels come out to do a quick wiggle.
Nature's own party, with snacks on the ground,
A feast for the critters who make merry sound.

So let's raise a toast to this verdant delight,
Where laughter and joy take glorious flight.
In a world so hilarious, don't be aloof,
Join in the fun, get out from under your roof!

Verdant Dreams in Quiet Corners

In the quietest nooks, where shadows play,
The green carpet beckons, come out and stay.
A turtle in slippers, a hedgehog in style,
They lounge in the soft, and they ponder a while.

A butterfly's gossip floats high in the air,
While ants trade their secrets without any care.
Whispers and chuckles weave stories anew,
In this wild haven where laughter grew.

Who wears the best outfit? It's hard to decide,
With leaves for a dress and a twig for a ride.
A cricket's chirp sets the rhythm of fun,
While the lizards join in, basking under the sun.

Watch out for the snail, oh what a slow race!
He glides with great style, keeps a steady pace.
In the tapestry woven of dreams and of cheer,
Every corner's a party – come join us right here!

Echoes in the Evergreen

In the depths of the woods, surprises unfold,
Where trees have their secrets and stories retold.
An owl wears spectacles, wise beyond measure,
He chuckles at antics that bring him such pleasure.

The bushes are bopping, a merry old crew,
With flowers that dance in a colorful hue.
A fox in a beanie, so sharp and aloof,
Cracks jokes with the sparrows, undaunted by proof.

Oh, the echoes resound with each playful breeze,
As nature's comedians giggle with ease.
They share in the tales of life's silly spins,
Like raccoons wearing masks as they search for their sins.

So if you should wander where evergreens sigh,
Tune in to the laughter, hear nature's reply.
In this bright tapestry woven so funny,
Every sound is a giggle; every giggle is honey!

The Cloak of Nature's Touch

A blanket of green drapes the old oak with flair,
While squirrels hold council, planning with care.
With acorns as snacks and jesters all around,
Their chitchat's a whirl, a conspiratorial sound.

The plants wear their cloaks, the funniest threads,
With tags from the bumblebees, stitching in reds.
A frog sings a ditty, all silly and spry,
'Life is a joke, come laugh with the sky!'

Each pebble's a dancer, soft moss on the floor,
Invites you to step, come waltz through the door.
The critters unite for a grand charade,
As whispers and giggles make the whole glen parade.

So let laughter loom large under nature's soft cover,
Frogs will be croaking, and blooms will discover.
In a world full of joy, where humor kicks in,
Join in the shenanigans, let the fun begin!

Textures of Tranquility

In the woods, my thoughts run free,
Lumpy carpets beneath the trees.
I trip and stumble, laugh aloud,
Become one with the forest crowd.

Bright green hats on fungi sprout,
Nature's quirks, there's never doubt.
A snail smiling, it takes its time,
This outdoor life feels so sublime.

Ants on parade in perfect line,
Each one thinks it's doing fine.
Life's a dance in earthy threads,
While we chuckle, the world treads.

The Harmony of Humus

Underneath the leafy flair,
Worms are having some wild affair.
They wiggle and giggle, who knew?
Soil parties, this must be their brew.

The crickets roam with grand designs,
Chirping laughter in earthy shrines.
Twirling beetles with jazzy moves,
Earth's disco ball, it surely groves.

Mice in costumes, oh what a sight,
Dressing up for a forest night.
Nature's jesters, never shy,
With silly antics, they amplify.

Elysium Underfoot

A stroll through greens, my heart delights,
Dancing blades in gentle fights.
Rose petals blush with secret glee,
While bees hum sweet, a symphony.

Twirling leaves in playful swirl,
Acorns drop like tiny pearls.
Grass tickles toes, oh what a game,
Each step proves the earth's never lame.

Ladybugs with polka dots,
Cruising round in funny slots.
A squirrel pirouettes off a stone,
What a show for those who've grown!

Musing Amongst the Greenery

Amidst the thickets, laughter swells,
From twigs it breaks, like joyous bells.
A frog croaks jokes in rhythmic tone,
While sunbeams tickle every stone.

Porcupines throw a pointy bash,
With laughter loud, they make a splash.
Their quills don't stop, they're on the go,
Punchlines sharp, just like their show.

In this realm where whimsy reigns,
Nature spins with playful gains.
Join the fun, forget your woes,
Amongst the green, comedy flows.

Tranquil Treads of Time

Upon the path where slugs do roam,
I often ponder, should they have a home?
With slime as their guide, they slide with grace,
Yet all I can see is their gooey trace.

A turtle stumbles, takes a wild spin,
"Just training hard for a race to win!"
But little does he know, it's a slow trot,
He's fashionably late, but that's not his plot.

The birds up high laugh at my shoes,
"They clash with the leaves, such terrible views!"
But I just smile, my heart's light and free,
For I dance with the bugs, and they dance with me.

So here's to the path that bends and twirls,
Where laughter and silliness make my heart whirl!
Through the trees and the trails, with cheer I will roam,
Living ever so boldly in my nature-filled home.

Ferns and Fantasies

In the shade of fronds, I find my muse,
Tickled by thoughts, like tiny shoes.
A ladybug winks, it's all in good fun,
"Come join me on this leaf, we'll bake in the sun!"

With each playful breeze, my worries slip away,
"Do ferns hold secrets?" I ponder and sway.
The squirrels chime in, their chatter so sly,
"Got tails of our tales, just watch as we fly!"

The mushrooms form meetings, oh what a sight,
Debating the best way to grow in moonlight.
"Should we wear hats, or tiptoe with flair?"
They break into laughter, it fills the cool air.

So let's post up here, in this green carnival,
Where everything sings, and nothing feels small.
With whimsy as our guide, life's a delight,
In a world of ferns, we'll dance through the night!

Nature's Gentle Embrace

Beneath a soft blanket of leafy green,
I chuckle at squirrels who act like they're keen.
"Where's all the acorns?" they flail and collide,
While I sip my tea, they stumble beside.

The brook gurgles softly, a bubbly old chap,
"Let's race to the bend!" "You're just taking a nap!"
With pebbles as spectators, they cheer and they peek,
While frogs croak some tunes, oh so forward and cheek!

A butterfly flutters with a wink and a nod,
"Do people know I'm a fashion icon, oh God?"
She twirls in the air, with colors that gleam,
While bees buzz around like it's all a dream.

So here in this wonder, I sit back and smile,
At nature's quirks, it's truly worthwhile.
Each laugh shared with critters, my heart feels so light,
In the arms of the wild, everything feels right.

Green Tapestry of Thoughts

A carpet of emerald spreads far and wide,
Where thoughts tumble 'round like a quirky wild ride.
The dandelions giggle, "Please don't pull us out!"
We'd rather blow wishes and dance with a shout!

The ants hold a meeting, their suits oh so neat,
Plotting their paths like a secret elite.
"Shall we take the long route or zoom through the grass?"

While a cat takes a nap—"Just let the day pass!"

The clouds gather 'round, playing tag in the sky,
"Who says naps aren't fun?" says a wink of a fry.
I'm lost in their game, their fluffy delight,
As I sit and enjoy, everything feels bright.

So let's weave the laughter into earth's tapestry,
With whimsy as we walk, so wild and so free.
In every green crevice, where humor ignites,
Life dances in joy—what a marvelous sight!

Nature's Quiet Narratives

The trees gossip softly, no need for a shout,
Their branches are waving, like they're having a bout.
A squirrel in a tux, with a nut for his snack,
Claims he's the king; who will challenge his pack?

Underneath the green, a snail set his pace,
He dreams of adventures, in this slow-motion race.
While flowers debate which color looks best,
A dandelion wins, and they all get distressed!

The Language of Luminescence

Fireflies chat, with flickers and darts,
In a waltzing display of glowing arts.
They throw a light party, with no need for sound,
While frogs in the corner offer croaks that astound.

The moon spills a secret, all quiet and bright,
As shadows conspire to plan their delight.
The night blooms with laughter, at stars in their jest,
Who twinkle and giggle, in their heavenly best.

Revelations in the Underbrush

Amidst tangled ferns and undergrowth wide,
A hedgehog debates, should he run, or just hide?
A busy ant brigade, with their mission so bold,
Argues about treasure, but it's all just old mold!

In this lively scene, there's much to uncover,
As worms trade their stories, debating raw cover.
A spider spins tales, on a silken string,
While beetles break dance, claiming they own spring!

The Comfort of Soft Textures

A carpet of clover invites little toes,
While a playful breeze carries secrets it knows.
The moss is plush seating for a tired old bug,
Who sips on sweet dew, feeling snug as a hug.

Fluffy seed pods whisper, 'We're ready to fly!'
While kittens in grass give their best meow-cry.
The world is a cushion, soft laughter rings clear,
As nature's soft textures wrap round us with cheer!